Truth
& other musings

Saana Allie

BookLeaf Publishing

India | USA | UK

Presentation by *BookLeaf Publishing*

Web: www.bookleafpub.com

E-mail: info@bookleafpub.com

ISBN: 9789360941390

First edition 2024

I write for those unafraid to delve into the deepest parts of themselves to discover the light in their lives. And, as always, everything I create is lovingly dedicated to the cherished people and animals that color my life with joy.

ACKNOWLEDGEMENT

My first anthology of poems is a dedication to the profound relationships that have molded me. To my dear family and friends, your love, the hurdles we've overcome, and your steadfast support have guided me like stars; to the animals that have graced my life, you've schooled me in the art of being present, the virtue of loyalty, and our quiet connection with the natural world. Together with all who face each day as it comes, we navigate the rich spectrum of emotions, unearthing the universal truths that reside within us all.

PREFACE

As I neared the end of writing a book that delved into the themes of war and conflict, I was enveloped in an intense storm of emotions. Love's gentle caress, hope's delicate glimmer, sorrow's deep ache, and fear's cold grip laid the foundation for the poems within this collection. This journey, rich with unexpected twists and deeply personal revelations, mirrors the unpredictable nature of writing itself.

Each poem is a sincere reflection, capturing fleeting moments and enduring experiences that have imprinted themselves on my soul.

Thus, it seemed only natural to embody this rich tapestry of feelings through an equally diverse array of poetic forms and structures. My hope is that these poems not only resonate with you but also illuminate the shared truths of our existence. I hope my words resonate with you and spotlight the universal truths of our lives...or at the very least invite you to explore your own emotional landscapes and find safety in our collective ability to persevere and find love and strength even in the midst of life's most daunting trials.

Truth

In this World of many Truths-each stands alone
My Truth is mine, your truth thine.
"Truthiness," by the way, is in the dictionary shine
When it should be in the Twilight Zone.

Where once singular Truths were the thread,
Guiding beliefs we could easily chart,
Now this plureality of life drives us apart,
Leaves us wandering, isolated, filled with dread.

Some hide the irritation, others take it in stride
And hope to reclaim Truth, for which we pine.
Imagine that, not yours, not mine,
But a World in which we might all reside.

Kandiaronk

Kandiaronk.
(I had never heard of him—I would have remembered a
Name that looked like a forest).
He was absent from my late-night readings of the
greats—
Voltaire, Rousseau, Montesquieu, Diderot, Kant—
(Immanuel & I share a birthday!)

Kandiaronk.
Years passed (centuries went by) before we met
A bold warrior, his mind as sharp as a knife,
A statesman with wit, in debate,
(I imagine his laughter, echoing with life).

He saw Europe with discerning eyes,
(Their ways, their follies, under open skies).
He questioned their structure,
Pitied their poor and their old,
Saw their stories untold,
Witnessed their lust for the gold
(His people's way was communal, he remarked,
"We leave no one in the cold).

His critiques, like water, flowed and reshaped
A stunned Europe; it could no longer dither
(You can imagine they did not like this man, this mirror)
Some thought his words were too sour
(Weak men will get angry and their faces will turn dour)
Yet some saw light amidst the darkest hours,
Wondering what was the worth of their divine powers
(Especially when greedy men live in ivory towers)

Kandiaronk.
It's true (and terrible) that I'd never heard the name,
(But his thoughts were all around me, in my
Constitution even, all the same)
If the Enlightenment was Europe's candle,
He may have been the flame.
(I wonder who else my history books didn't claim).

Running from race

In America, the issue of race cannot be outrun
(I've tried, believe me, so many times, in vain)
Woven across this historied, hysterical land,
The same inquiries in this melting pot:
"Which ingredient are you?"
"Check all that apply."

It's omnipresent yet unspoken.
Those people topple statues, the others raise scary
flags with ease,
Everyone is obsessed with symbols, ignorant of
meaning, unbothered by history.
(How did South Africa do it? Germany?
Can someone help stop save us)

A tiring marathon, this race about race,
I don't have the shoes for it, no one has the words
The hateful ones are awful but please don't rely on the
self-proclaimed saviors
(Who hang their hat on BIPOC hiring behaviors)
BIPOC, what a way to say "not white"
(A fact too uncomfortable to say in a
so-called safe space)

Once upon a fairly recent time, I would not be hired
Because of my skin
Now I uncomfortably wonder if it's the reason
I'm taken in.
Either way, when you're a token,
Expect to get spent.

Shahenshah

Under Syria's skies, so vast and deep,
A Shia lord roamed, denying himself sleep.
Through the bazaars and alleys, his vigil he kept,
And even the stars in reverence wept.

His court would question, "Why forsake thy bed,
When golden chambers call thee to repose?"
Yet he, in nightly vigils, softly said,
"A ruler's heart must feel his people's woes."

"For if a single soul in my domain,
Man or beast, in sorrow doth remain,
How can I rest, when duty calls me hence,
To soothe their woes, and be their strong defense?"

Thus, through the night, his path of mercy went,
A king of kings, on love and kindness bent.
In history's scroll, his tale of empathy,
Shines through the ages, for all eternity.

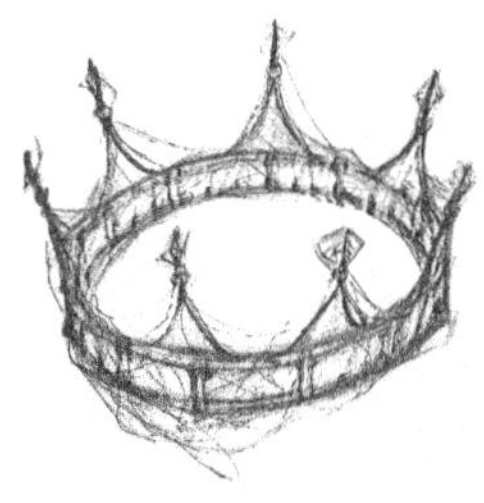

Not great, Britain

In the mournful dusk, cruel lines were drawn,
By distant rulers, with hearts so cold and vain.
Lahore to Delhi, a sacred kinship torn,
Severed roads bleed under Britain's reign.

With one brutal stroke, Britain cleaved apart,
Hearts entwined in history's tender vine.
Tears like rivers flowed, daggers pierced every heart,
On altars of haste, a ruthless, tragic line.

From Punjab's weeping fields to Bengal's cries,
Even today hears the screams of partition's plight.
Millions torn from home, under anguished skies,
A civilization's soul, shattered in endless night.

In each silent sob, the earth bears deep scars,
Legacy of pain, beneath the Partition's stars.
Families shattered, dreams forever marred,
In every broken heart, the past's cruel disregard.

A chasm of sorrow, so profound and vast,
In the shadow of Britain, history's most cruel villains
cast.

Not your Middle East

In the grandeur of the Waldorf Astoria's time-honored
hall,
Where nations' voices echo, rise and inevitably fall,
An American girl, curious and bright,
Queried the Chinese Ambassador under the
chandelier's light.

"Why 'Middle East,' when to you, it's west?"
She mused, putting history's words to the test.
Each sat with an old-fashioned in that opulent space,
Where every corner whispered elegance and grace.

The diplomat, a hint of mischief in his gaze,
Spoke, "In China, we're the 'Middle Kingdom,' always.
Yet we use terms of others, maps of distant lands,
A nod to history's flow, a shifting of the sands."

"But let me share," he continued, a clever twist in his tone,
"This matters more to you than to us, it's known.
We're more for the practical, the concrete and real,
While you ponder the words and their superfluous appeal."

The girl's gaze sharpened, her lips curved in a downward smile,
"Now that's an idea to sit with, I'll ponder for a while."
In the heart of the city, amidst the splendor so rare,
She mulled over his words, in the grandeur there.

One day in Gaza

One day in Gaza, someday, there'll rise,
A monument 'neath sparkling blue and safe skies,
In a park where flowers will blush and trees shall sway,
You'll see a testament to what was once an
Inconceivable type of day.

There it will stand, some kind of calendar, a guide,
Or perhaps a sundial, basking in pride,
And carved on its surface, these words will display:

"Here, on such and such day,
All was fine, all was okay.
No soul passed, no heart bled dry,
No injustice even tried to shadow the sky.
Just a normal day, in every way.
May we always have such unremarkable types of
days."

We found them at dusk

We found them at dusk, these camps, these museums
of miseries.
Tents battle in the wind, clinging to earth with their
weary inhabitants.

We are human, all woven from the same thread.
I think, every soul here once nurtured dreams.

A mother weaves old tales into a girl's hair.
A boy too young for an aged gaze, stares at an empty
plate.
Something inside me irreparably breaks.

Here people hover between despair and hope.
Afraid of both.
The air is thick; expectant and resigned.

It is quiet. Eerie. Only babies scream.
They haven't learned yet there is nothing they can do.

In these silent galleries, ghosts of what was linger.
Lands that began humanity belong to no one any
longer.
Shame burns within, for those who feel none.
For those who look away, are far away.

I look up to hide the tears (like molten sorrow) as they
fall. Above, past these stolen lives, the stars stand
witness.

These eyes of distant, unfeeling gods.
Still better, I think, than us, who look away, though we
carry uneasy hearts.

What worth is an outcry, how powerful is it even?
What even is the sound of fury, if not a soul-shattering,
swallowed cry.

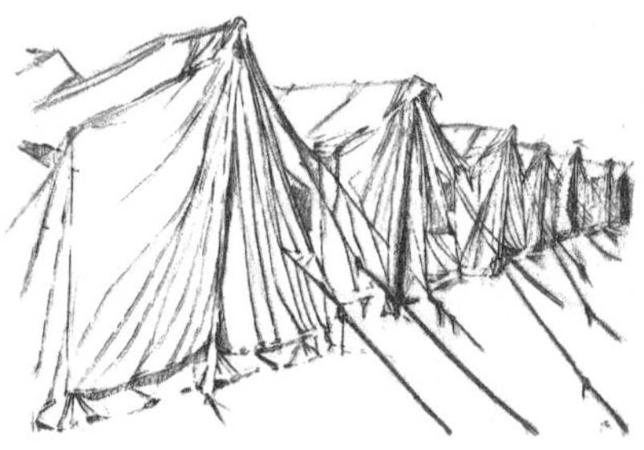

lol

Tyrants tremble at the jest,
Satire's sharp blade, hidden, rests,
Silenced laughter in the air,
Echoes truth they cannot bear,
In whispers, freedom's test.

Moscow5

"Have you heard of Moscow4?" Navalny quipped with glee,
His eyes, deep and blue, sparkled with mischief's light.
"No, what's that?" we asked, intrigued by the mystery,
Ready for a tale to fill the room that night.

Navalny's seriousness faded, and Alexei took center stage,
His laughter rang out, such a bright and joyful sound.
He shared a story, from the intelligence page,
Of a password saga, where folly was found.

"Well, the email of the very top brass guy from intelligence
was hacked several time
and his first password was Moscow1
and they hacked him so his second password was Moscow2
and they hacked him as well, so the third time
he had Moscow3 and just guess what was his fourth password...
Moscow4!
so Moscow4...
is the explanation for the stupidity of the system."

And then the tone, it shifted, became somber and grave,
The day they sentenced him, hoping he'd fade away.
We went back to that moment to get away from that dark day

They wanted him silent, in the cold, a forgotten knave,
Yet in that moment of cruelty, his spirit didn't sway.

Wrapped in lies, for speaking truths so bold,
Of a Russia reborn, from the ashes of the old.
In his cell of ice, his heart never turned cold,
They imprisoned Navalny but Alexei laughed at them,
his defiance uncontrolled.

As the end approached, his laughter filled the air,
A sound of triumph, in the face of despair.
"Blind they are, to think this is fair,
But in the echoes of time, I'll always be there."

For Alexei, the laughter lingers on,
A bittersweet reminder, after he's gone.
In the fight for truth, his spirit won't be pawned,
For this is the tale of Moscow5, where his legacy is
drawn.

Lost, Together

I see her before she sees me
I knew her before she knew me

She walks with her head bowed, treading lightly,
respectful of us departed souls,
Tracing names etched on stones until she finds mine
I feel her weight come to rest by my feet
Oh how I have waited!
In death, I have watched and waited her whole lifetime
for this moment

"Salaam nana-ji," she says
"It took a long time to find you but I found you"

Walaikum salaam meri jaan, I say

She doesn't hear me
She never hears me

She pulls out a small jug and two cups
"I made chai for you," she whispers, a shy smile
Like all the girls in our family

"I don't know very much about you," she speaks so
softly
"But I love what I know;
That you were an orphan, and people were so cruel to
you but they never won;
That you and nani-amma were so in love;

That you couldn't read but you had a photographic
memory;
That you built an empire for us."

As she recounts my successes, her own voice gets
stronger

"But I also know you hated if your daughters wore
their hair down," she laughs like a bell
From my perch, I've watched her smile light up rooms
and bring others to ease
"And mama says if you had been alive, you would
never have let her marry a Shia"

I wince
It's true, I say
*But none of that matters, I see so much more from
here*

She doesn't hear me
She never hears me

"Nana-ji, do you know no one in our family knows what
to do with me"

Her shoulders hunch, her spine slumps

"They used to scold me and say I was just like you,
stubborn, opinionated, argumentative
I just couldn't let unfairness go
And I think they meant it as an insult but I would think,
I'm like my grandfather
So I did it more"

And then, my girl with the mighty heart and gemstone
eyes begins to weep
Weeps at my feet!
And I curse the gods for keeping me from lifting her
head high with my hands
My once-hands, turned ivory turned dust

"I don't know what to do, I'm so lost
I think I can do these big things and I can't, I keep
failing
Everything has gone wrong
So so wrong
And I'm so alone here"

I hear her gulp for air, I send her a strong wind

A light mist of rain falls over her
For I am crying too

It's okay, I say
You will be okay, I promise
I see so much more from here
You open your heart to all the horrors of this world,
things others flee
You have still never learned to ignore unfairness
You never can
You are the one in our family charged with the task of
feeling everything
It is the cost of being the one who can fix everything
You understand things so quickly but my darling you
must also see
You are not perfect
But you are not alone
You don't have to be perfect

She doesn't hear me
She never hears me

The rain falls harder, thick gray drops crash into her
skin, into our chai
Her dark shawl cannot keep out the cold
Right now, she does not believe she even deserves
the warmth

I watched her think so many times she is not enough
Other times she fully believed she's too much
But now, she doesn't believe anything
And this
This emptiness is the worst thing she's ever known
Her emptiness is the worst pain I've ever felt

Across the veil, I try to ease her spirit

In every darkness you have, I am there too, I am the
light
Every time you fall and you somehow find the strength
to stand again,
That's me, bringing you back into the fold
I exist in a place beyond what you can know
I am here
I see so much more from here
I will always help you back up, back inside from the
cold

She doesn't hear me
She never hears me

She doesn't hear me when I beg her not to absorb too
much pain
She doesn't hear me when I explain why I wanted my
girls to be taken care of
She doesn't hear me when I plead with her to be safe
She doesn't hear me when I marvel at her courage to
face her demons
She doesn't hear me when I say I am filled with pride
That if there must be a world that makes girls have to
be this brave
That I am so proud of being the grandfather to the
bravest one
Better than all the boys

She covers her face with her hands
Her body wracked with pain
She has not cried like this in a long time
I know because I have seen it all, watched all of her
old selves

The girl who swam before she walked
The one who learned to read early as a child
The one who learned to listen early as an adult
The one who has been so polite with her sadness
Is the one shattering into pieces at my gravesite

Shhh, meri jaan
Breathe
You have been afraid and alone before
This will pass, too, maybe not soon
Maybe it will take you years to talk about things

Maybe you never will, maybe this you will keep secret
This depth of pain you feel now will be matched by the
height of joy you have yet to know
The duality has to exist for any of it to have any
meaning
I see so much more from here
My love, the time will come when you will be proud of
getting up again, from this highest fall,
And the power behind your steps
That will be me

She won't stop crying
She can't stop crying

Am I helping? Is this helping her?
All I want is to hold her

She was born in a monsoon
She is not afraid of a storm
These days she is afraid of the people she once
trusted

My sweet girl, my child's child
I see so much more from here
The place where you belong will not exist until you
build it
You will find people who never let you feel alone again
Picking yourself up from where you are now will be the
heaviest weight you've ever lifted
Keep going, keep going

She looks up
The wind brushes her hair away from her eyes for me

She doesn't know it but she is looking straight into
mine

You must rest now, my lovely one, for many days
I know they hurt you but they did not break you
Like me, you, are made from a wood that does not
burn easily
You will not be the same after this pain nor should you
be
Change looks beautiful on you
Go to your home, across the seas where I sent my son,
Let others care for you, do not hide your sadness
Part of being a friend is letting others be a friend to
you
I will be there too

Through the magic of the Divine, I sense something
steadying within her
The first seed of nourishment has been planted

She empties the cups of the chai we did not drink,
smoothes the soil that rests above me
She sits for endless moments then rises

"I love you so much" she says through trembling lips
To a grandfather she has never met,
And will not meet for many years yet

I love you too, I say to this luminous being in a world
that often dims,
I love you more than anything
Our hearts break and mend at the same time
The world has its miracles
And you are mine

She walks an unsteady path

Keep going, keep going, I say

She doesn't hear me
She never hears me

How am I?

Stop. Just stop.
I know what you're going to say.
You'll ask how I am and I will want to break away.

Don't. Don't you dare.
How do you think I can play this game, win this fight?
You'll want me to fib, say something lie-t.

Leave. If positivity is what you want, please leave.
I do not have anything except my skin and bones.
I cannot comfort you with dulcet tones.

But stay, if you can, and offer warmth.
The antidote to grief isn't denial;
It's the feeling of a friend holding your hand for a while.

Sit with me, I cannot be alone.
Help me learn like Atlas, how to carry these boulders,
On my hunched-over, fragile, weak shoulders.

The Ballad of Softened Rage

In shadows cast by towering might,
Where silence speaks and fear takes flight,
Women learn to tread with steps so light,
To cloak our roar, keep rage from sight.

We yearn to be the fierce dynamite,
That cleaves through stone, against the night.
Yet, find we must, a path more slight,
Become the stream, in soft moonlight.

This rage within, a fire bright,
Must cloak itself, in gentle plight,
Bending, twisting, through the fight,
Like countless women lost to sight.

Within us burns a wish to write
Upon the sky, in strokes of white,
Yet, we must dance with shadows tight,
And voice our truths with whispered might.

RBG

They scoff at her—our mighty Ruth—
Blaming her for everything terrible (*ever*)
She, who toiled for liberty and truth,
From the earliest days, compassionate and clever

Methodically, she wove change's lace
With a pen that spilled irrefutable reason
(At a steady, strategic, tireless pace)
Yet some *(you know who)* scream, as is their wont in
any season,
To always demand more and more *(and yet from her,
wish less?)*
They couldn't Garland the court, don't even bother to
mention that,
Nor did they do anything to prevent the disastrous
mess,
*(They actually happen to be regular contributors to the
tension)*

I hear this opinion often (luckily never from a close
friend)
I smile and nod in such discussions *(#fruitless)*
The brilliant woman worked until the very end
And departed a sad state, leaving us Ruthless.

DC on the rocks

In DC's swirling social whirl,
Where drink is king and ice cubes swirl,
The cautious soul stands out, so stark,
Amidst the merry, tipsy lark.

"Why not a drink?" they often probe,
In this city, full of lights that strobe,
My choice, in day and night is to stay sharp and clear,
To see the world without the goggles beer.

There are corridors of power, steeped in wine,
Where deals are made over dine and brine,
And in these rooms a clear head is a rare find,
In the hustle, the daily grind.

They can't fathom why I might sometimes abstain,
In a culture where to refrain
Means you've lost and then regained,
Some harrowing sobriety, from depths that need not
be explained.

But here I stand, amidst the cheer,
Choosing not to bend to pressure *a la* peer,
For clarity, not out of fear,
In a city that struggles to see what is near and dear.

So let them think what they will,
As they sip and seek their thrill,
I'll navigate this festive spill,
With my own kind of skill.

It's not a battle, nor a plight,
But a choice to embrace the night,
With senses sharp, and insight bright,
In DC's endless, dizzying might.

A good cry would have sufficed

There once was a tale, not of love, but of woe,
A lesson in mental health from Romeo.
Had he just shed a tear,
Instead of acting in fear,
They'd both be alive, not below!

One less than you

In a debate lively and great,
One was calm, the other irate.
"Of gods, there's quite a few,
I happen to believe in just one less than you,"
Quipped the skeptic, to set things straight.

Aneri

*A*mber light in laughter's cozy glow,
*N*ightingales serenade as she strolls slow.
*E*vening breezes whisper secrets she'll decode,
*R*adiant calm, where wild dreams are stowed.
*I*n her, a whimsy world finds its abode.

The Mountain's Secret

Not with force, but flow,
Water shapes the stone below,
Softly, we shall go.

Love Languages

In tongues diverse, love's essence is arrayed,
"Doret begardam," Farsi's tender serenade.
Words that in English, find no counterpart.

"Merak," in Serbian, where passion's cascade,
"Koi no yokan," in Japanese, love's prelude laid,
In tongues diverse, love's essence is arrayed.

"Saudade," Portuguese, of longing's shade,
"Yuánfèn," Chinese, fate's intricate braid,
Words that in English, find no counterpart.

"La douleur exquise," love's French masquerade,
"Geborgenheit," German, where trust is weighed,
In tongues diverse, love's essence is arrayed.

"Mamihlapinatapai," Chilean, unspoken, never frayed,
"Ishq," Urdu whispers, in devotion's parade,
Words that in English, find no counterpart.

These words, love's deep mysteries never fade,
In every language, love's uniquely made,
In tongues diverse, love's essence is arrayed,
Words that in English, find no counterpart.

When our love was complete

When our love was complete—and I mean,
Really-truly-no kidding-there is gone all doubt
I quietly fetched my notebook, the one with the blue roses
Your sister gifted me ages ago, now all worn and stout.

Before I could write anything, the page filled
With the splatter of a teardrop
I wiped the slate clean, and in defiance I willed,
A list of places where we had been happy.

At Martin's Tavern, the Kennedy booth,
Do you remember?
We celebrated your birthday early that first year
Since I wouldn't be home until November

And the little wildlife sanctuary,
Where behind the labyrinth of branches
We found a bench as sweet as you please
Where I would pretend to scoff as you would tease

And of course, in Georgetown, where we would stand
Admiring the lights dancing on the river.
That one night, the storm froze us on sidewalk,
You refused the taxi,
Embraced, in this order: life, the rain and me.

I revisited all our places, over a few months in time
To take what once felt holy and ours and
Make it wholly mine

To revisit these old haunts, places I want to
Always love and adore
Knowing I will never sit with you there again,
Not anymore.

I had to do this, you see, to break your hold
And still cherish these places that bring me peace,
manifold
I go often to these spots alone or with friends, glad for
the places I can still revere
Even if our own love, now complete, is no longer here.
Why we fell apart quickly became clear;
I saw the truth with relief, without fear.

There was such sadness but a revelation divine
Only when we were at the end, did we ever rhyme.

Xerxes

In the tapestry of life, where threads intertwine,
Xerxes, is my compass, every moment of mine.
With fur like the dawn, caressing the day,
And eyes that lit paths in the most enchanting way.

Together we stood, a duo so bold,
Him and I, too many stories to be told.
His presence was a fortress, in the silence of the war,
A promise that always together, we would soar.

Xena and Leonidas echo his might,
In their courage, their whimsy, in the calm of the night.
In every sweet animal I rescue and share our space, I
catch a glimpse of my boy, I feel his grace.

He wove confidence into the seams of my soul,
With him by my side, I felt capable, assuredly whole.
His spirit was a beacon, through turmoil and fray,
Let me know that everything would be-
and it wasn't over until it was-
Okay.

His eyes saw a world where fear found no ground,
In his last days, in his knowing eyes peace was found.
His departure, thus, became a lesson in facing the
end,
With an acceptance so few comprehend.

I read all the books in his absence, searching for a
belief,
Anything, anything that could offer relief.
How naive I was, so ignorant of such grief.

In his last seconds, I promised him this,
I spoke these words and sealed them with a kiss:

*"My sweet, darling boy,
Thank you for trusting me to keep you far from pain,
And when I leave this world too,
I will roam the cosmos, I will find you again."*

tim russert did not make a sex tape.

"no no no no no no no no"

agonized the aunties (not knowing
i under the kitchen table was playing)
with my new-found rock (smooth/shiny/black) from the
street

"you cannot let her do it"
eyes widened, teeth sucked

"it's for her English," mother's voice
(nervous yet defiant) floated down to me,
"i've seen the show,
they are men of a certain age, looking so serious,
dressed so uncomfortably!
what har(a)m could they possibly do?"

"nonononononono"

(a barrage of gunfire)

"you've just arrived (months ago), you don't
understand," decried the aunties,
"amreeki tv's all haram—
sex, killing, drugs, alcohol...
these americans (they love recording the sex)"

mother gasped (twice) and coughed for air

"really? is this true?"

aunties, satisfied (spreading fear in my mother),
mollified (shifting to nuanced tones),

"you know, you must watch with her"

they spoke of me (as if i wasn't there)

"just to be sure it's okay"

and so, that sunday, mother brewed chai
the scent of cardamom strong (not as strong as her
glare at an unsuspecting tim russert)

"meet the press," mother sounded out
(maybe also her way to learn angrezi?)
"okay, let's meet them"

tim russert did not make a sex tape.

not that sunday, nor the following ones (mother
watching closely)
i learned English:
bipartisan, nafta, sanctions, dot-com, a newt gingrich

sometimes, months later, she'd burst in,
as if to catch him (in the act)

tim russert did not make a sex tape.

instead, he did what the little girl suspected (and the
grown-up confirms)
was (far) more scintillating:

holding politicians' feet to the fire, grilling them,
extracting truth or admissions of wrongs

before angrezi, i learned the power of the press,
(i got to meet them) at my kitchen table

Whales

Majestic,
Through ocean's vast sweep,
Gentle giants glide,
In their ancient, graceful dance,
Wandering.

A Painter's Night

In shadows' dance, by candlelight, I paint,
My brush weaves dreams, in hues so faint.

Each flicker casts a world unseen,
In the soft glow, colors convene, by candlelight, I paint.

The night whispers secrets, old and quaint,
In this quiet hour, no restraint, by candlelight, I paint.

Canvas listens to the flame's complaint,
Stories emerge, a saint, a quaint, by candlelight, I paint.

In every stroke, a whisper's faint,
A dance of light and shade, my soul's quaint, by
candlelight, I paint.

Oh, in this solitude, no feint,
True colors bleed, my heart's acquaint, by candlelight, I
paint.

Let the dawn wait, in its ascent,
For now, in candle's glow, I'm content, by candlelight,
I paint.

www.ingramcontent.com/pod-product-compliance
Lightning Source LLC
LaVergne TN
LVHW021305200726
843509LV00012B/1787